W9-BYJ-172

3 4028 08777 6861
HARRIS COUNTY PUBLIC LIBRARY

J 177.7 Pon
Ponto, Joanna
Being kind

$22.60
ocn900665806
10/15/2015

WITHDRAWN

Being Kind

Joanna Ponto

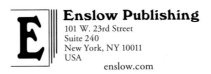

Enslow Publishing
101 W. 23rd Street
Suite 240
New York, NY 10011
USA

enslow.com

Published in 2016 by Enslow Publishing, LLC.
101 W. 23rd Street, Suite 240, New York, NY 10011

Copyright © 2016 by Enslow Publishing, LLC.
All rights reserved.

No part of this book may be reproduced by any means without the written permission of the publisher.

Library of Congress Cataloging-in-Publication Data

Ponto, Joanna, author.
Being kind / Joanna Ponto.
    pages cm. — (All about character)
Summary: "Provides character education through different scenarios that demonstrate children being kind"—Provided by publisher.
Audience: Ages 4-6
Audience: K to grade 3
Includes bibliographical references and index.
ISBN 978-0-7660-7116-2 (library binding)
ISBN 978-0-7660-7114-8 (pbk.)
ISBN 978-0-7660-7115-5 (6-pack)
1. Kindness—Juvenile literature. 2. Conduct of life—Juvenile literature. I. Title.
BJ1533.K5P656 2016
177.7—dc23
                        2015000154

Printed in the United States of America

To Our Readers: We have done our best to make sure all Web sites in this book were active and appropriate when we went to press. However, the author and the publisher have no control over and assume no liability for the material available on those Web sites or on any Web sites they may link to. Any comments or suggestions can be sent by e-mail to customerservice@enslow.com.

Photo Credits: Aigars Reinholds/Shutterstock.com, p. 16; Ben Bloom/Photodisc/Getty Images, pp. 3 (right), 6; Bob Marmion/Shutterstock.com, p. 18; David De Lossy/Thinkstock, p. 22; Elena Elisseeva/Shutterstock.com, p. 8; Jupiterimages/Pixland/Thinkstock, pp. 3 (left), 4–5; kali9/E+/Getty Images, p. 14; KPG Payless2/Shutterstock.com, p. 1; Olesya Feketa/Shutterstock.com, p. 20; Rob Lewine/Getty Images, p. 10; Ryan McVay/Photodisc/Thinkstock, pp. 3 (center), 12.

Cover Credit: kali9/E+/Getty Images (boy and girl playing soccer).

Contents

Words to Know

kind   recess   shovel

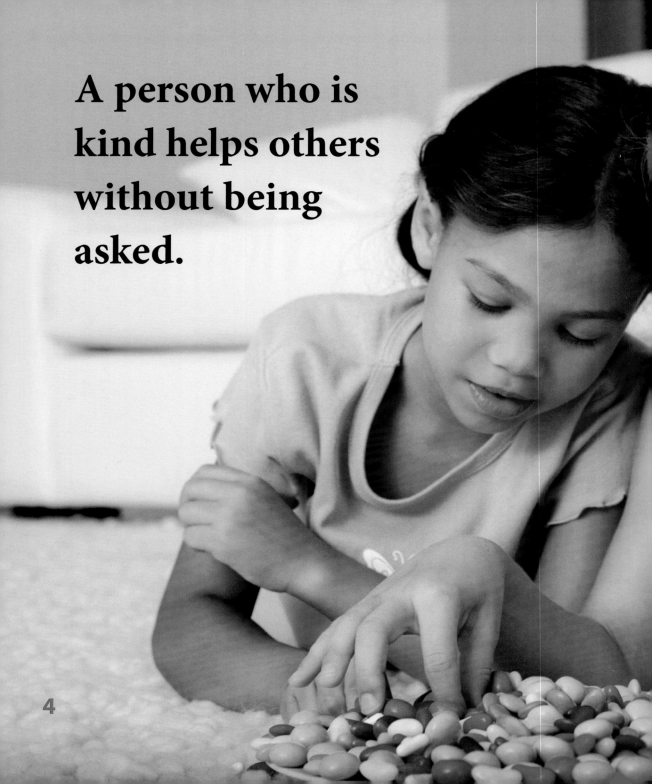

A person who is kind helps others without being asked.

4

A person who
is kind shares.

5

Lee's neighbor is old.
It is hard for him to
shovel snow. Every winter,
Lee shovels his neighbor's
sidewalk. Lee is kind.

Lily saw her friend fall while rollerblading. Lily helped her get up. Then Lily helped her friend get home. Lily is kind.

Gabriel's friend lost his pencil for class. Gabriel gave him one of his pencils. Gabriel is kind.

There was a new girl at school. Kim asked the new girl to play with her at recess. Kim is kind.

Tyson is the best player on the soccer team. Chrissy is not as good as Tyson. Chrissy wants to get better. Tyson practices with Chrissy. Tyson is kind.

Susie's bicycle had a flat tire. Susie's sister Amy let her borrow her bike. Amy is kind.

Leo's sister Anna is saving money for a new video game. Anna sells lemonade to earn money. Leo helps her sell it. Leo is kind.

Juan was on his laptop. His little sister wanted to play. Juan played a computer game with her. Juan is kind.

Kyle lost his dog. Hope helped Kyle look all around the neighborhood. They found his dog. Hope is kind.

Read More

Lennon, Liz. *I Am Kind.* North Mankato, Minn.: Sea to Sea Publications, 2012.

Woodson, Jacqueline. *Each Kindness.* New York: Nancy Paulson Books, 2012.

Web Sites

Sprout: Kindness Counts
  sproutonline.com/kindness-counts

Kids for Peace: Community Builders
  kidsforpeaceglobal.org/pro_community.html

Index

Guided Reading Level: C
Guided Reading Leveling System is based on the guidelines recommended by Fountas and Pinnell.

Word Count: 208

Harris County Public Library
Houston, Texas